All You Need To Know About

Writing Brilliant Dialogue

by

Philippa Carron, PhD

Wild Goose Publishing

Wild Goose Publishing

A Division of Yelsel International Pty Ltd
PO Box 9174 Deakin ACT 2600 Australia

The moral rights of the author has been asserted.

This edition published by Yelsel International Pty Ltd, Canberra, trading as Wild Goose Publishing

National Library of Australia Cataloguing-in-Publication data:

Author	Carron, Philippa
Title	All You Need To Know About Writing Brilliant Dialogue
Edition	1st
ISBN	978-1-925474-01-5
Subjects	Writing fiction, creative writing, novel, literature, dialogue

Disclaimer

About the Author

Philippa (Pippa) Carron, PhD, is a free-lance writer, editor, trainer, workshop facilitator and personal writing coach. She works for a range of private sector and government clients, delivering writing courses and providing high-level writing and editing services through her company Yelsel International Pty Ltd, under the business name Writing in the Gap (www.writinginthegap.com).

Pippa's writing experience includes academic papers, theses, conference papers, speeches, handbooks, training manuals, procedure manuals, workbooks, technical books, PowerPoint presentations, government reports, issues papers, précis, business plans, magazine articles, travel articles, promotional flyers, and brochures. More recently, she has been working with fiction writing, editing and manuscript appraisal, and leads a creative writing group. She is a member of the Australian Society of Authors, the Canberra Society of Editors and the ACT Writers Centre. She lives in Canberra with her iPhone, iPad, Apple MacBook Pro with Parallels, and two desktop PCs.

NOTE TO INTERNATIONAL READERS

The author of this publication is Australian and therefore follows Australian standards for grammar, punctuation and spelling. Australian standards generally follow those of the United Kingdom. Major discrepancies in writing and editing style between Australian English and American English have been noted in this publication and it is thus suitable for a global audience.

Contents

Preface

So you're writing a novel? Congratulations! You're in for loads of fun.

Story-telling is an ancient art and creative fiction is one of the most satisfying pursuits of all time. It has many advantages. Unlike the visual arts, you do not need paint or brushes or clay or a studio to work in. All you really need is a pencil and paper, or of course an electronic way of writing, and the strong desire to tell a story. What's more, you can work on your story anywhere, any time: while you are in the shower or doing the dishes, you can be thinking up devious plot twists; while travelling on a bus or train, you can be taking notes about the looks and mannerisms of the people around you; while you walk or drive, you can talk into recording software on your smartphone; while you have conversations with friends and family you can get ideas for dialogue; and while you watch television or movies, you can get ideas for scenes and sequels.

There is, of course, far more to creating a *publishable* work of fiction than just telling a good yarn, and this book is aimed at giving you the tools you need to write excellent dialogue, a vital part of any work of fiction these days. This book has been brought together to give you not only the essential theory, but practical examples so you can truly understand what is required.

This text has drawn on examples from the works of other writers. Wherever these examples occur, a shorthand reference is provided in the text with full supporting references provided in a bibliography which can be found at the end of this book. Occasionally, I have used passages from my own fiction writing where published examples were not readily available. These citations are obvious by their lack of a source reference.

Chapter 1

The Role of Dialogue

Dialogue is a vital element of fiction and its role is always more that just two or more talking heads. As well as progressing the plot, it can provide information about:

- the character who is speaking (e.g. *'I don't give a stuff about what she thinks. She's just a little twerp.'*)

- other characters who are present (e.g. *'I love the way you look in that purple dress.'*)

- other characters who are not present (*'She flew home to Darwin on the midnight horror.'*)

- the setting (e.g. *'The lake was full last time we were here.'*)

- action as it is happening (e.g. *'Run faster Harley.'*) or not (e.g. *'Come on Rita, wake up.'*)

- the tone of interaction between characters (e.g. *'Hello sweetheart, you look beautiful tonight.'* versus *'How dare you walk into the house in those muddy boots.'*)

- reveal theme (e.g. *'We can't let them suffer that way just because they're animals.'*).

Dialogue is also an excellent opportunity to provide humour, especially through sarcasm or wit from a particular character known for that way of speaking and, in this way, to lighten the pace or change the narrative tone.

When writing dialogue, examine each statement made and critically appraise it as to what its role is and whether it is absolutely necessary. Dialogue should not provide information that has already been provided in narrative elsewhere, or by other people in their conversations, unless it is integral to plot or character exposition.

Chapter 2

Characteristics of Good Dialogue

Dialogue Isn't Real Speech

Writing good dialogue is definitely an art. Dialogue has to give the illusion of real speech. That is, it must sound natural, not wooden. It mustn't sound 'preachy' or like a lecture, unless that's your intention and then it needs some subtle explaining. However, while it has to sound natural, dialogue in fiction is usually an abbreviated form of how people normally speak. It is more compressed and purposeful.

On one hand, dialogue has to sound as if people really are talking to each other. Yet on the other hand, it has to be pruned of all the superfluous words and vocalisations that people usually utter when they are having a conversation. (Have you ever noticed how often people, especially women, say 'hmm' while another person is speaking?)

Typically, dialogue makes considerable use of word contractions to make it sound casual (e.g. don't, can't, should've, hasn't, it's, he's, she'll). Notice the difference between these two pieces of dialogue.

- 'I do not think she will be able to manage it on her own. Let us help her,' he said.

- 'I don't think she'll be able to manage it on her own. Let's help her,' he said.

However, you can take advantage of the common use of contractions in conversations and not use them when you want someone to sound formal. For example:

- 'She should have started walking by now,' he said.

- 'You do not have my permission to look at that book,' she said.

Another nuance of dialogue is that many common words spoken by people in conversation are left out, unless absolutely necessary to the context. These words are mostly adverbs and adjectives (e.g. just, actually, really, very, simply), so do get rid of these types of words.

Similarly, get rid of all the little words that start conversations, such as 'well', 'yes', 'no', 'like' and 'so'. Also do not put in words that are not normally used when people are speaking, but are normally used in prose. The best example of this is the word 'that'. In grammatically correct prose we would write, for example, 'The dog that I saw crossing the road ...', but in dialogue it would be 'The dog I saw crossing the road ...' or perhaps, more colloquially, 'This dog I saw crossing the road ...'.

Individualised Character Voices

Dialogue is the emotional powerhouse of your character interactions with each other. If your plot is the bones and your narrative the muscle, then your dialogue is the blood that pumps the energy around the body of your story.

In the broader sense, the 'voice' of a character is the *essence* of them, it is their mannerisms, the way they think, their level of education, the impact that their social environment has had on them, their confidence and self-esteem, their goals and aspirations, and the way they see themselves in the world. In short, it is the character's personality that comes through when they speak. John Marsden believes voice is so important in fiction that he starts, not with plot or setting, or the factual details of a character's life, but with his or her voice.[1]

People reveal themselves in overt and covert ways when they speak and so your characters should be individualised by the voice you give them in their dialogue, both in what they say and how they say it. This can be quite difficult to do, but the type of distinctions you can make lie in:

---

[1] *Everything I know about Writing* by John Marsden (1993) p.129.

- whether they are men or women (men tend to get to the point, solve problems and present facts while women like to build relationships and talk about emotional matters)

- their age (e.g. child, teenager, young adult, thirty-something, mature aged, elderly)

- their degree of formality (e.g. they don't speak in contractions) or informality (e.g. they use colloquial words, slang and swear words)

- their level of education/ignorance (revealed by the their vocabulary)

- whether they are immigrants or non-immigrants

- whether they are indigenous or non-indigenous people

- their socioeconomic status (e.g. upper-class versus lower-class in historical novels)

- whether their overall attitude is positive or negative, accepting or suspicious, etc

- their level of confidence, overall and in given situations

- their level of experience in a certain situation, versus a complete novice

- their use of humour, especially sarcasm

- sentence length (e.g. long rambling sentences or short, sharp, declarative sentences)

- whether they are brief or loquacious (i.e. verbal diarrhoea)

- the idiom, colour, rhythm and idiosyncrasy of how they speak

- how opinionated or judgmental they are, especially about other people and situations

- their degree of certainty and authority or vagueness

- if they have a non-English speaking background they are likely not to use correct English syntax (e.g. *'I am thinking you going to the shops.'*)

- diction and enunciation of words (e.g Uriah Heep in *David Copperfield* by Charles Dickens always said *'umble*)

- their use of peer-group jargon (e.g. gang mobs) or technical language (e.g. doctors)

- whether they speak in vernacular or with accents

- whether they swear or blaspheme and, if so, how often.

- whether they are very precise or imprecise in their statements

- whether they are loud, persistent, keen to make themselves heard and interrupt other people or get spoken over or interrupted all the time

- their use of repeated filler words (e.g. like, actually, really, just, generally)

- their inclusion of other character expressions (dialogization).

You can also use dialogue effectively to break stereotypes; for example, the female psychiatrist who swears giving evidence in a courtroom; the hacker who talks as if she has a PhD in Old English Literature; the Australian Aboriginal man who speaks with an Asian accent; the young Chinese woman who speaks with a strong South African accent.

When they are first introduced, your characters' dialogue may not reveal much about their backstory, deeper motives, fears and anxieties, but it should start to reveal key aspects of their personality: their class and education level, outer persona and preferences. What impressions do you get about the characters who make these statements?

- She stood beside him, her arm brushing his sleeve. 'My father returned to Cambridge for two years. On the way home we visited Paris.' ... 'I've imagined,' she confided to him, 'that I'll go back one day and claim Paris for myself. It's been a kind of promise.' [*Conditions of Faith* by Alex Miller, p.6]

- "And now," Bruce went on, "suddenly you're putting all these new initiatives on the table. Low-flow plumbing. A complete carbon inventory. Temperature setbacks. Guert, where is this crap coming from?" [*The Art of Fielding* by Chad Harbach, p. 59]

- —For this, O dearly beloved, is the genuine Christine: body and soul and blood and ouns. Slow music, please. Shut your eyes, gents. One moment. A little trouble about those white corpuscles. Silence, all. [*Ulysses* by James Joyce, p.1; note, Joyce uses a dash instead of dialogue marks]

- I stopped her. "No, no," I said. "I'm in a hurry. I'll take them as they are." [*We Need to Talk About Kevin* by Lionel Shriver, p.4].

- Call Judith, he said over his shoulder. She's been trying to get you all day. Your mother's dead. [*Dirt Music* by Tim Winton, p.165; note, Winton does not use dialogue marks].

- You wanted to know what the bad guy looked like. Now you know. It may happen again. My job is to take care of you. I was appointed to so that by God. I will kill anyone who touches you. Do you understand? [*The Road* by Cormack McCarthy, p.61 of 225; note, McCarthy does not use dialogue marks].

The voice that you select for your character must be authentic. This is a tough one to understand at first because 'authentic' often implies true to a stereotype, whereas the last thing you want in your story is stereotyped characters. By authentic we mean true to the character that you have created. For example, a child must behave and speak like a child, unless they have been created to behave and speak in a much more mature way; and then, if they have been created more mature than their age, they must behave that way always, unless there is some reason why they are being more childish than they normally are (and this reason must be explained in the narrative). Here is an example of a British child who has been created by the author so he speaks like an adult. The child, Edward, is about five years old, and the adult is a man in his thirties, Guy Perron.

'Who are you?' the boy asked.
'I'm just a visitor. Who are you?'
'I live next door. Is that my ball?'
Perron stooped and showed it to him.
'It looks like mine. Has it got MGC on it?'

Perron inspected it. 'Yes, you can just see MGC.'
'Then it must be mine. MGC means Mirat Gymkhana Club. Mr McPherson always used to give me used tennis balls. '
...
'You're Edward are you?'
'Yes. My full name is Edward Arthur David Bingham.'
My name's Guy Perron.'
'They are both rather funny names, but I like Perron best. So I'll call you Perron'
'Then I shall probably have to call you Bingham.'
'Okay.'
[*A Division of the Spoils*, Book 4 of *The Raj Quartet* by Paul Scott, p. 502 of 599]

Here's another example of a precocious child, this time seven-year old Sophie is talking with her father (the story's protagonist) whom she sees irregularly.

'So – where shall we go then?' he asked Sophie.
'Don't mind.'
'Well, what do you feel like eating?'
'I like sushi,' said Sophie showing off.
'You don't like sushi.'
'Yes I do,' she said, but without much conviction.
'You're meant to be a child Sophie; children don't like sushi. Not even Japanese children.'
' Well, I do. Sushi and sashimi.'
'So when do you have sushi then?'
[*The Understudy* by David Nicholls, p.119 of 408]

Dialogue Beats

Dialogue is often inter-dispersed with short pieces of descriptive prose (called dialogue beats or action tags), about character actions to show how a character is behaving as the dialogue progresses. This mimics real life, where people are often performing a task or moving in some way while they are talking. In fiction, dialogue beats can be a great way to tie characters into a setting, keep the action going, and impart essential information through the conversation. Here's an example.

As his father stopped the ute and turned off the engine, Ben turned to Louise. "Let's get working."

Louise helped unload the tools and wire. "It's such a shame the homestead has become so rundown. It would have been beautiful when people lived here."

Ben agreed. Full of energy, he hefted the metal star pickets over to the yards and leant them against the rails. "Yeah, but then we wouldn't have a park, and we wouldn't be catching brumbies."

Mr. Naylor went through the gate and kicked one of the posts. "You haven't caught any yet. This place won't hold a legless donkey, let alone a bunch of wild horses."[2]

It's become very fashionable to remove dialogue tags and replace them with dialogue beats. Here are some examples of where a tag has been turned into a beat.

Tag	'What about?' asked Nick, pulling a white shirt out from his pack.
Beat	Nick pulled a white shirt out from his pack. 'What about?'
Tag	'What's up Blue?' said Jeremy as he held Nick at arm's length after they'd hugged. 'You look like you've been hiking a road back from purgatory, not holidaying in Goa.'
Beat	Jeremy held Nick at arm's length after they'd hugged. 'What's up Blue? You look like you've been hiking a road back from purgatory, not holidaying in Goa.'
Tag	'Where's Nick?' asked Hilary, looking around at the crowded room. 'I do hope he's OK. It would be so easy for that cut to get infected.'
Beat	Hilary looked around at the crowded room.

---

[2] *Brumbies* by Paula Boer, p.30 of 140. Note, this book has been written entirely without dialogue tags, relying completely on dialogue beats to let the reader know who is speaking.

	'Where's Nick? I do hope he's OK. It would be so easy for that cut to get infected.'
Tag	'Hilary's had her PhD conferred, so she's a doctor now too,' said Dan, putting his arm around her shoulder and kissing her on the temple.
Beat	Dan put his arm around Hilary's shoulder and kissed her on the temple. 'Hilary's had her PhD conferred, so she's a doctor now too'.

The main problem with dialogue beats is that they can get too long, or too frequent, and interfere with the flow of the conversation. If there is too much narrative about what each character is doing while they are speaking it becomes hard for the reader to follow the conversation. The same thing can happen if too much thinking state or deep-third prose is inserted between dialogue beats to reveal character emotions. Here is an example of a conversation where a considerable amount of both action and deep third prose is inserted between each person's dialogue beat.

She dropped her hands in amazement, or maybe shock. Brady couldn't seriously mean that, could he? "I can't do nothing. They can't start their married life with Alex hiding another wife. Even if she isn't really his wife. It's ... it's ... wrong."

He spread his arms and cocked his head in a very French gesture. At least it looked French. Or Italian. The "What's the problem? And I don't want to get involved" gesture. "Why not? Couples have all sorts of secrets. They lie to each other all the time."

"No they don't!" He was serious. And what sort of people did he mix with? The loose-living, jet-setting Mediterranean yacht owners?

He turned away, muttering. "My parents did. They lied to everyone. Each other, themselves, me, the police."

Phoebe bit her lip. Anger and astonishment subsided rapidly, replaced by a surge of sympathy. This was a different thing altogether. The bitterness in his voice and gesture said it all, an emotional exposure he probably rarely allowed, or was unaware of. "Do you see them, your parents?"

[*The Wedding Party* by Elizabeth Rose, Loc:221 of 2192]

Now if your intention is to reveal character thoughts and emotions, this type of dialogue is fine, as long as it is not overdone. If your intention is to have two people talking intermittently, inter-dispersed narrative can work well too. But if you are writing a fast-paced thriller, then you might want your dialogue to be a bit more snappy.

Another problem is that you can end up with a repeat of names, as shown in the fourth example above where Hilary's name has to be put in twice. Be careful, also, when you replace dialogue tags with action beats that you don't end up with a confusion as to who is actually doing the talking. Here's an example:

Dan hugged Katie. 'Oh, we miss you guys so much.'

We don't actually know whether Dan or Katie says 'We miss you guys so much'. In this instance you would need to write:

Hugging Katie, Dan said, 'Oh, we miss you guys so much.'

Which isn't wonderful, so it might be better to put the action beat and dialogue tag before the dialogue:

Dan hugged Katie and said, 'Oh, we miss you guys so much.'

Dialogue beats are essential when silence is being portrayed. Rather than writing something like *She didn't reply* or *She stayed silent*, you can add in a physical response, but do ensure that the physical response gets its own line, just the way a beat of dialogue would. Here's an example.

She retraced her steps beside the lake, back across the crunching gravel, and around the sharp curves of Commonwealth Park to Regatta Point. And there on the grassy bank below the flagpole sat Nick, cross-legged, eyes closed, forearms resting on his knees, palms up. Gold wedding ring glinting in the sun.
'Hi Katie,' said Nick with eyes still closed.
'How did you know ... ?'
'I saw you from the other side of the lake when I was running there a while ago. And as you came by, I could smell that perfume you always wear.'
She felt so foolish, standing in her tennis whites. So much for no-one knowing where she was. She must have stood out like

Macquarie Lighthouse on Dunbar Head. She started walking again, quietly, so he wouldn't hear.

From a few paces away she heard him say, 'I'll walk back with you, if you like.'

She turned, expecting to see he'd started walking too, but he was still sitting there, smiling in Western Buddha bliss.

'Or maybe you could join me?' he said. 'I've always thought you'd enjoy transcendental meditation.'

Finally, the sequence of dialogue and dialogue beats should also follow the standard sequence of stimulus→reaction→action. This mean that something happens, the characters reacts to it internally, then either says or does something. The following sequence is thus incorrect:

'I can't see anything,' William said as he looked intently into the mist after hearing a fog horn sound in the distance.

To be correct it should be (noting that the dialogue tag can be omitted with this sequencing):

A fog horn sounded in the distance. William looked intently into the mist. 'I can't see anything.'

Chapter 3

Creating Compelling Dialogue

Creating Conflict and Drama

In genre fiction, you should think of dialogue as 'action in words'. The best dialogue occurs when two people are diametrically opposed in their goals and are each pushing their own agenda, though this doesn't have to be done bluntly. Before writing each scene that contains dialogue, get clear in your own mind what each character's scene goal is and ensure that at least two are in opposition. If they aren't in opposition, then it's likely that there's no need for the dialogue. The fact that they agree can simply be put in narrative text. For example, the following dialogue:

> Lucy said, 'I'm going to the hairdressers on Thursday to get my hair cut short.'
> 'Short?' said Millie. 'How short?'
> 'Real short, like a boy's crew cut.'
> 'Oh, right. Where will you get it done?'
> 'There's a new place in town, at the back of the arcade.'

could be simply:

> Lucy went to the new hairdressers in the arcade and had her hair cut short, really short, like a boy's crew cut.

or better, the next time Lucy and Millie meet, Millie says:

> 'OMG! A crew cut? What possessed you to do that?'

Once you have the potential for confrontation set up in your dialogue, you can ramp it by:

- having one of the characters start to do something that's known to be annoying to the other

- turning the argument into a screaming contest or fight

- introducing an internal barrier, such as one of the characters refusing to talk any more or walking away

- introducing an interruption to a delicate conversation at a crucial moment.

- introducing an element of fear for one or both characters.

However, if your characters aren't sufficiently different, or have different goals, then you are going to struggle to write dialogue that contains sufficient interest and tension to sustain your readers. So remember, scintillating dialogue emanates from brilliant characterisation. Even if this just means ensuring your characters have some quirky aspects that come out in their dialogue.

As well as ensuring you have conflict, there are several tricks you can use to make your dialogue more interesting. The first is to play with text reversal. Here's an example of reversing text, with the original text followed by a reversal of words to stop the dialogue being so stereotyped and to make Dan sound like he was trying to be funny.

ORIGINAL: Dan picked up Baby Hugh with a proud, fatherly smile and made formal introductions. 'Hugh, this very intelligent man is Clive and this very beautiful lady is Katie.'

REVERSED: Dan picked up Baby Hugh with a proud, fatherly smile and made formal introductions. 'Hugh, this very beautiful man is Clive and this very intelligent lady is Katie.'

Another trick is to break up the dialogue at a key point with some action. For example:

'So what sort of things do you tell her?'
'How you're the pin-up boy among the rich and famous in Maui. How you teach all the sexy female graduate students to ... hey, there's a taxi.' He ran out onto the edge of the road and waved it down.

A third method is to use side-step dialogue, when you insert a completely unpredictable or random statement into the dialogue of one of your characters. For example, the following conversation is somewhat mundane:

'So how's your day been?'
'Oh OK.'
'How's your new boss behaving?'
'She's OK.'

Now let's spice that up with a little side-step:

'So how's your day been?'
'Oh OK.'
'How's your new boss behaving?'
'Did you go out with Nancy last night?'

Creating Dialogue Subtext

Often what your characters don't say is more interesting or important than what they do say. Alternatively, they might say one thing while they obviously mean another thing. The revealing of meaning through cryptic dialogue or through contradictory dialogue beats is called subtext.[3] It's also sometimes called a person's 'hidden agenda'.

A good example of subtext in dialogue is where a couple is arguing over a trivial matter while avoiding talking about a more serious matter. Another example is where a character makes herself busy to avoid a conversation. A third is where one character is left clueless because she is not told what she should be told which will engender a feeling of sympathy from the reader. And yet another example might be an internet date where each character is twisting the truth about himself or herself. Topics that are a good source of subtext are: past relationships; secrets; past crimes, fears and hopes, bad experiences, enemies, and vivid childhood memories.

The key with subtext is the reader should subtly pick up on the disjunct between what the character is doing versus what they are saying, or what the character is saying versus what they should be saying (i.e. they are lying). When done well, the reader will pick up the true emotion that underlies the character's behaviour. In this

---

[3] Dialogue subtext is a subset of the much broader topic of narrative subtext.

way, subtext is a useful to set mood and create tension in dialogue, as well as show what is important for each character.

Along with an understanding of subtext goes the caveat that people rarely speak in a completely open and heart-felt way about their feelings. Because this rarely happens in real life, it can sound artificial in fiction. The way around this is to add subtext through physical actions or facial expressions which might be contrary to the way a character is speaking (e.g. *She dropped her briefcase on the floor and slumped in the nearest armchair. 'Yeah, yeah, I'd love to go out to dinner.'*).

Avoiding an Info Dump

While dialogue is obviously a clever way to drop in pieces of information that are key to plot development or characterisation, it shouldn't be used as a mechanism to dump large amounts of information. Here's an example of info dump in dialogue.

> Tynan slapped his hand down on Jack's wrist and wrapped his fingers around like a tourniquet.
> 'Why d'ya do that?'
> 'Because you told me you weren't interested in Brenda and now I find out that you've been going out with her for a month. You never gave me a chance. She'd only just broken off with me. She said she wanted to take a break. She said I could ask her again in a few weeks. And now I find out you asked her out the very next day.'

Oh no, whoa! Would a man who was angry with his best mate talk like that? Say so much in one long speech? Let's run that one past again.

> Tynan slapped his hand down on Jack's wrist and wrapped his fingers around like a tourniquet.
> 'Why d'ya do that?'
> 'Because you're a bastard.'
> Jack tried to pull his wrist away. 'I'm not a bastard. Let go.'
> 'You should be tortured for what ya did.'
> 'What? What did I do?'
> 'You've been going out with Brenda '
> la de da ...

Yes, it's going to take a bit longer to get the information out, but it's a lot more realistic. Don't forget, if there is lots of action happening, and good dialogue, a reader will wait quite a while to find out why the action is happening the way it is, or why the characters are saying whatever they are saying! In fact, this is a good way to create mystery and suspense.

Avoiding Idiot Lectures

Dialogue also shouldn't be used to feed in exposition that the reader doesn't yet know, but which characters should already know. Termed an 'idiot lecture', this is another newbie writer mistake. For example:

> Mary: 'Darlin', I wish I was coming a huntin' with you.'
> John: 'Mary, this trip is going to be a tough one. I need you
> to stay home at our ranch at Beaver Rock to look after our
> two boys Merv and Dyson. But thanks for coming as far as
> Runaway Bend to see me off.'

In this example, there is no need for John to mention their sons' names, their property name, or even where she is stopping (Runaway Bend). These sorts of details, if necessary, need to be worked into the narrative in some other way. If the boys names are essential, then find a way of individualising them. For example:

> John: 'Mary, I need you to stay home to look after Merv seeing
> he's been so sick and to make sure that Dyson keeps the cattle fed.'

So when assessing your need for dialogue, make sure that your protagonists are not going to say anything that they both already know, with the notable exception where a crime is being discussed and two characters are comparing facts, though these facts should be ones the reader doesn't know, and the scene should lead to some divergence, where one person has a fact that contradicts another's understanding, or where new facts are being revealed by one person which the other and, importantly, the reader doesn't know.

Similarly, dialogue should not provide information that the reader can work out for herself. Indeed, this is the trickiest part of writing dialogue: to provide hints to the reader as to what is going on, without revealing too much. This is especially vital in thriller and crime genre, but also plays a strong role in other genres, such as romance and chick lit.

Avoiding Preaching

Along with info dump comes 'preaching' because that is exactly how a character can sound when the author is trying to use dialogue to articulate part of a moral premise, convey a theme, or hector another character. Here is an example from some of my writing where a manuscript assessor said I was 'preaching'.

> She crumpled then, as a wave of emotion washed right over and he held her hard while sobs convulsed her shoulders.
> 'Beautiful?' she asked again when her catharsis was over.
> He sat down. 'If you like, I'll make a recording of me saying it over and over. But I'd put other things in the recording.'
> She sat down beside him. Rubbed her swollen eyes. 'Like what?'
> 'Like that somewhere along your journey over the last few years you got lost and now you're not sure who you are. That you were probably forced to be someone you weren't by your parents and you rebelled, but your rebellion has now become counter productive. It gave you a persona you enjoyed at first because it was so outrageous and confrontational, but now you resent it because you feel trapped. That while you're covertly proud to be gay, you also think there's a possibility you're not gay, that you're bisexual. I certainly thought you were when we danced together last year.'

While I didn't particular agree with the assessment as it was in my character's nature to be the sort of person in whom other people confided, and I did want to keep the paragraph, I addressed the criticism by adding two lines (underlined below) which gave him permission to be 'preachy'.

> She sat down beside him. Rubbed her swollen eyes. 'Like what?'
> <u>'You really want me to tell you what I think?'</u>
> <u>She nodded.</u>
> 'Like that somewhere along your journey over the last few years you got lost ...'

You can have your characters have intellectual discussions[4] and make speeches, but there must be a purpose to it and they must be interesting and well crafted.

Adding Protagonist Commentary

Sometimes dialogue needs protagonist commentary, and this is usually done in thinking state or deep third. Here are some examples from *Journey to the Stone Country* by Alex Miller.

> He didn't move. 'You afraid of this feller?'
> 'No,' she lied, meeting his gaze steadily. [Loc: 708 of 4636]

> 'I wouldn't mind going back to the Suttor one of these days just to have a look.' It was not what she meant, but it would have to do for now. The reality was too complicated . There was too deep an ambivalence in her attitude ... [Loc: 830 of 4636]

> She had said 'yes' but it had sounded more like 'no'. 'Of course I want to see them,' she said quickly. But all the same she was not sure. ... She was not ready. [Loc: 1074 of 4636]

> He stood breathing. 'I'll get it later.' His voice was husky and low, as if he confided some shy knowledge of himself that he was unwilling to speak of openly to others. [Loc: 868 of 4636]

> 'Do you ever go back to the Suttor country?' she asked
> He didn't look at her. 'I've been back,' he said.' [Loc: 1011 of 4636]

> 'That would be wonderful,' she said, and knew it was not the response he required. [Loc: 1074 of 4636]

> Bo said, 'I'll have something for you in a minute there, Mister White,' He spoke as if he and the cat had already discussed the matter of tidbits from the fish. [Loc: 1370 of 4636]

> 'Them trees have always been there,' Bo said, offhand, as if the ancient trees were not subject to the years as man is and their ages

---

[4] For example, Paul Scott, author of *The Raj Quartet*, was an absolute master at creating intellectual discussions between his characters. In this way he was able to examine in considerable depth the theme of colonial imperialism in India. Another great example is Winston Graham in his 'Poldark' series.

could not therefore be calculated by such a measure. [Loc: 1968 of 4636]

There was a tightness in his voice suddenly, as if speaking of this matter he was moved by an apprehension or an emotion that he had not anticipated. 'The time's never been right to have a go at it before this.' [Loc: 2471 of 4636]

'Oh I don't know!' she said with sudden impatience, hearing herself talking as if she were back in Melbourne with Steven and their friends ... [Loc: 2471 of 4636]

'Don't worry. I'm not going back to him,' Annabelle said. She was surprised by the assurance with which she said this and wondered if it were true. [Loc: 3093 of 4636]

Chapter 4

Conveying Culture in Dialogue

Accents

We live in a multicultural society and a cosmopolitan world. Many of the characters we have in our fiction speak English with an accent, either as a native tongue (e.g. Scottish, Irish, American Australian) or as a foreigner who has learned English as a second language. It is very tempting to try to write accents into dialogue but it is almost impossible and does get tiresome for a reader. Here are three solutions.

First, state in the dialogue tag that the person speaks with an accent. For example:

'Except that I'm not Cockney,' said Prescott, exaggerating his Canadian accent. 'And he's a millionaire.'

Second, you can drop in the occasional vernacular word to remind the reader that the character comes from another country and thus speaks with an accent. For example:

'Jings,' said Hillary. 'He's a wee bonny baby.' [Scottish accent implied]

Third, use an ungrammatical construction that is characteristic of non-English-speaking people. For example:

Kalpesh beamed with an inscrutable smile. 'For me it is happy day. One year ago, I am thinking my Masters no good. But academics I am meeting in Brisbane helping me and I get Masters done. Then Sydney professor helping me get tutor job. My wife and little girl daughter coming soon from Goa. So now happy, happy, happy, not boring, boring, boring. And thank you all for invite me to conferencing again in your very very nice Kombi bus.' [Kalpesh is Indian]

By all means, use these tricks, but don't overdo it!

Vernacular

Dialects and vernacular refer to the words that various cultures use that are specific to those cultures and particular includes idiom, euphemisms, slang, jargon. Like accents, vernacular is hard to create convincingly in fiction and readers do tire of it quickly. I recently re-read *Lady Chatterley's Lover* by D. H. Lawrence and while I enjoyed it immensely, the vernacular dialogue was hard going at times. Here is an example:

> When he came back she was still lying there, glowing like a gipsy. He sat on the stool by her.
> 'Tha mum come one naight ter th' cottage afore tha goes; sholl ter?' he asked, lifting his eyebrows as he looked at her, his hands dangling between his knees.
> 'Sholl ter?' she echoed, teasing.
> 'He smiled. 'Ay, sholl ter?' he repeated.
> 'Ay!' she said, imitating the dialect sound.
> 'Yi!' he said.
> 'Yi!' she repeated.
> 'An' slaip wi' me,' he said. 'It needs that. When sholt come?'
> [D H Lawrence *Lady Chatterley's Lover*, loc: 2779 of 4766]

Australian author Tim Winton writes much of his dialogue in an Australian vernacular, and with no dialogue marks.

> Take you to Broome if you shout me the juice.
> Fox shrugs. Orright, he murmurs. Spose it'd give the trip some shape.
> Shape. Yeah. That's what I'm after. I'm gunna get shaped up in Broome.
> Yeah? How's that?
> [Tim Winton *Dirt Music*, p.230]

While this type of language conveys a strong sense of the way a certain class of people talk in Australia, I suspect that Winton's readership is limited by the fact that many international readers might fail to understand or appreciate the heavy use of Australian vernacular, or not want to read it.

Use dialects and vernacular sparingly and only for strategic purposes. Give the reader a taste of it early on, then pull back. If you have described your character appropriately, then the occasional reference to the character's physical attributes will also help remind the reader that they are from a foreign country or speak in a particular way.

Eras

If you are writing in any era other than the present, you will need to be mindful of not using words that are inappropriate to the era. This doesn't mean that you have to use words that were current at the time but which are no longer used now (e.g. the language used by Chaucer or Shakespeare), but you should not use words that were obviously not current in that era. The maxim is to be as neutral as possible with your choice of language.

If you do want to make your language authentic, research how other high-profile authors have handled language specific to your particular era. Read books, letters and journals from that period if possible as well. Letters, particularly, can give you a feel for how people spoke at the time and place where your novel is set. Then drop some similar phraseology into your dialogue. Here is an example from *Caleb's Crossing* by Geraldine Brooks which is set in Massachusetts in about 1650 where both the prose and dialogue use period language, though only lightly.

> I had my hand on the door latch, hesitating. There was supper to prepare, and yet I did not want to interrupt the teaching, nor could I get about the kitchen with so many bodies in my way. I was struggling to keep my composure, and felt I might give way at any moment. I turned, to go back out, but the master called my name and bade me sit. "I—I do not think—I need to be about my duties," I said, trying to speak in a natural voice. Caleb, whose back was to me, caught the agitation in my tone and turned. I have no idea how much of what I felt was disclosed in my face, but Caleb's gaze informed me that I did not look myself. He stood up and grasped my elbow, and steered me down upon the bench.

"Are you quite well?" said Master Corlett, all concern. "You look flushed—are you fevered?"

"It is nothing," I said. "A headache merely."

"My dear, please, go into my chamber and lie down up on the bed. I shall send a boy to the apothecary for a draught...."

"No, master, do not trouble a boy, there is no need of a draught." The apothecary charges a chouser's prices for draughts any goodwife could distill. I knew the master was not in purse to pay for such things. "But I will lie down for a while, if you can spare me."

[Geraldine Brooks *Caleb's Crossing*, pp.208-9]

Author of *The Secret River* and her accompanying story of how she wrote the book, *Searching for the Secret River*, Kate Grenville provides a whole chapter on her struggles to create convincing dialogue. She examines how other authors have handled dialect, vernacular and accents, and said her 'ah ha' moment came one day listening to E. Annie Proulx talking on the radio:

She said that she tried to make the order of the words convey the 'accent' or cadence, rather than spelling out the words phonetically. She used turns of speech and vocabulary that were distinctive to the characters, but sparingly. Sometimes she did use phonetic spellings, but only when it was a word we got used to seeing spelled that way—like 'git' for 'get'. A scattering of phonetic spellings and a lot of work on the rhythm of the sentence would give you an accent more seamlessly, she thought, than all the tedious stuff with apostrophes. [*Searching for the Secret River* by Kate Grenville, loc: 2608 of 2840].

Grenville's book is well worth reading if you are writing in a particular era, both for information on how to write appropriate dialogue, and how to carry out historical research.

Swearing and Blasphemy

Should your character swear? This important question can only be answered by you, the author, because whether your character swears depends on the type of person he or she is, and only you know that. But here are some general guidelines.

- Women generally swear less than men, but you can take advantage of this and have a female protagonist in a stereotypical role who behaves in a non-stereotypical way by swearing at inappropriate times (e.g. a female opera singer who swears backstage).

- Occasional swearing by a protagonist who never normally swears can add tension to a scene.

- You can use pseudo swearing, especially for characters with cultural associations with certain words (e.g. a London lad saying 'effing' all the time).

- You can allude to swearing by having a dialogue tag (e.g. *He would have sworn at the kid, but he knew Melinda hated men who spoke coarsely.*).

- You can use words that are common to the culture in which your fiction is set and are not considered to be swear words within that culture, but which might be considered swear words in other cultures (e.g. Australians frequently use the word 'bloody' and 'bastard' and it is not considered to be offensive).

Blasphemy is also something that you need to consider in relation to your genre and audience. Like swearing, it has the potential to offend and of course you would never use it in works aimed for publication in, for example, Christian romance titles.

If you do choose to use profanities (swearing) or blasphemy in your dialogue, do it very sparingly. They lose their shock value quickly and readers tire of seeing them if they are overdone.

Chapter 5

Dialogue Tags

Keep Tags Simple

A dialogue tag is the piece of text that lets the reader know who is speaking. It's also sometimes called a dialogue attribution. Dialogue tags should be kept to the basics of 'said', with a smattering of other verbs such as 'asked', 'whispered' and 'shouted'. This is particularly the case where dialogue can go on for a half page or more and the word 'said' rapidly becomes a 'white word' much like white noise. They slip into the background and most readers don't notice them. Note, when writing in present tense, the verb in the dialogue tag becomes 'says' (singular) or 'say' (plural). For example, *'I'm not going,' she says.*

However, a lot of well-known authors do use other verbs for dialogue tags, though they do it sparingly. These words include: added, announced, barked, blurted, called, chuckled, cried, croaked, demanded, enquired, exclaimed, exploded, giggled, growled, hissed, jeered, murmured, purred, questioned, scoffed, slurred, snarled, sneered, snickered, squeaked, recited, yelled.

To resolve this apparently contradictory state of affairs, my recommendation is, if you find you do want to use a dialogue tag other than 'said', first consider whether you can write the emotion into the words being spoken and, if you can't, then choose an appropriate alternative for the tag.

A similar dictate applies to adding adverbs to dialogue tags, with many writing technique purists declaring that it shouldn't be done: that the dialogue itself should convey the sense of emotion being expressed by the person who is speaking. So to avoid using an adverb, a verb phrase or clause is used instead of the dialogue tag which indicates the character's emotional state. Here is an example.

Poor	'I'm exhausted,' James said wearily.
Better	James slumped in the chair. 'I'm exhausted,' he said.
Better	James slumped in the chair and stared at the ceiling. 'I'm exhausted.' (i.e. no dialogue tag is necessary)
Better	James slumped in the chair and leaned his forehead on the table. (i.e. no dialogue is necessary)

Again, I've found that many well-known writers do use a range of descriptive adverbs to support dialogue tags. For example: she said ... quietly, loudly, grimly, haughtily, slowly, hesitantly, haltingly, wryly, sarcastically, slyly.

The bottom line is this: if you use verbs other than 'said' for dialogue tags, use them sparingly and only if you can't find a way of conveying the emotion in the dialogue itself. Ditto for adverbs which modify the dialogue tag verb.

Don't Use Action Verbs For Dialogue Tags

It's very tempting, and common among novice writers, to use other, non-speaking action verbs for dialogue tags (e.g. nodded, winked, smiled, laughed, giggled, waved). Here are some examples.

Wrong	'I like going to the zoo,' she smiled.
Right	'I like going to the zoo,' she said, smiling.
Right	'I like going to the zoo.' She smiled.
Better	She smiled. 'I like going to the zoo.'

Wrong	'She's coming with me,' he winked.
Right	'She's coming with me,' he said and winked.
Right	'She's coming with me.' He winked.
Better	He winked. 'She's coming with me.'

Omit Dialogue Tags

Once you've established who is speaking with appropriate dialogue tags, you can of course leave the tags off altogether. By doing this, you cut out unnecessary words and speed up the pace of the conversation for the reader. Here's an example:

> Her rubber-soled boots were silent on the path, but somehow Nick knew she was approaching. Maybe he'd seen her reflection in the chopper canopy or heard the terminal door closing. He turned and walked towards her.
> 'Hi Katie,' he said softly.
> 'Hi Nick.'
> 'I'm so sorry for what I said last year.'
> 'I'm sorry too. I was so rude.'
> 'But you were right. I was only thinking of myself.'
> 'But I had been so fickle.'
> 'But I'd never tried to understand.'
> 'Because I made you think I couldn't explain.'
> 'Some time, I'd like to know ...'
> 'Some time, I'd like to talk about it.'
> 'So how have you been, these last few years?'
> 'Oh, up and down. Sometimes it is a struggle ...'
> 'Same for me. There are days out on the ocean ... '
> ' ... when I think of you all day.'
> He opened his arms.
> She stepped towards him and he enfolded her in his big embrace.

However, you may come to the point where the reader gets lost in whose dialogue is whose. The answer is to add in some small actions, or dialogue beats, for each person, still leaving off the dialogue tag. Here's the same text with a few dialogue beats to help the reader keep track.

> Her rubber-soled boots were silent on the path, but somehow Nick knew she was approaching. Maybe he'd seen her reflection in the chopper canopy or heard the terminal door closing. He turned and walked towards her.
> 'Hi Katie,' he said softly.
> 'Hi Nick.'
> 'I'm so sorry for what I said last year.'

'I'm sorry too. I was so rude.'

'But you were right. I was only thinking of myself.'

She looked towards the end of the runway. 'But I had been so fickle.'

His eyes followed her gaze. 'But I'd never tried to understand.'

'Because I made you think I couldn't explain.'

'Some time, I'd like to know ...'

'Some time, I'd like to talk about it.'

He turned back to look at her. 'So how have you been, these last few years?'

She looked into his eyes. 'Oh, up and down. Sometimes it is a struggle ...'

'Same for me. There are days out on the ocean ... '

' ... when I think of you all day.'

He opened his arms.

She stepped towards him and he enfolded her in his big embrace.

While I personally prefer the former as it seems smoother and faster, you can judge for yourself which you think is better.

Confused Dialogue Tags

Along with eliminating dialogue tags comes the possibility of confusion about who exactly is saying what, especially when other information is included along with the dialogue beats. Consider the following exchange which happens after Josie hears her phone ring.

'Damn,' said Josie.

'I'll be back in a second Jim. I just need to take this call.' Josie walked a few metres away from the café and put the phone to her ear. 'Hello?'

'Mrs Spelding?' The voice asked. Josie let out a long, painful sigh.

'It's Ms Creen. I don't go by that name anymore.'

At the last line of this exchange, it is impossible to know who is speaking (is it 'the voice', or is it Josie?) because both 'The voice' and 'Josie' are referred to on the line above. There is also confusion because Josie speaks in the first and second lines of this exchange when her conversation should all be in the same paragraph. Here is a corrected version, plus a clarification about 'that name'.

'Damn,' said Josie. She called out to Jim, 'I'll be back in a second. I just need to take this call.' She walked a few metres away from the café and put the phone to her ear. 'Hello?'

'Mrs Spelding?' The voice asked.

Josie let out a long, painful sigh. 'It's Ms Josie Creen. I don't go by the name Spelding anymore.'

Here is another example of confused dialogue tags, plus some deep third thinking by Mandy which follows Craig's dialogue which adds to the lack of clarity about who is saying and thinking what.

'You're the love of my life.' Craig's tone was gentle and it made Mandy feel sexy.

'Is that what you say to all the girls?' Craig pushed the hair off Mandy's face and tilted his head to the side. He looked at her sweetly, innocently, lovingly. It made her heart melt.

'I have huge plans for us. We're going to be rich.' Rich in what, Mandy wasn't sure. But she trusted Craig. He was her husband after all.

And here it is corrected.

'You're the love of my life,' said Craig.

His tone was husky and it made Mandy feel sexy. 'Is that what you say to all the girls?'

Craig pushed the hair off Mandy's face and tilted his head to the side. He looked at her sweetly, innocently, lovingly. It made her heart melt.

'I have huge plans for us,' he said. 'We're going to be rich.'

Rich in what, Mandy wasn't sure. But she trusted Craig. He was her husband after all.

And here's a third example of confused dialogue.

'I need a loan,' Joan said in her most business-like voice. Zachary looked at her, waiting for more information. She didn't speak.

'What's the loan for? A house, investment or personal loan?' She cleared her throat uncomfortably.

'Actually, it's for a debt.'

'What kind of debt?'

And here it is corrected.

'I need a loan,' Joan said in her most business-like voice.

Zachary looked at her, waiting for more information.
She didn't speak.
'What's the loan for? A house, investment or personal loan?'
She cleared her throat uncomfortably. 'Actually, it's for a debt.'
'What kind of debt?'

As these examples show, you must make sure that it is absolutely clear who is saying what, even at the expense of adding in a few extra dialogue tags, action phrases or lines, especially where one person doesn't respond, as in the examples above.

Placement of Dialogue Tags

The careful placement of dialogue tags can make it easier for the reader to know who is speaking. Consider this example.

'No, we have all sorts of professionals talk at our conferences who look at social and economic factors that impact on the environment so we can do some sort of cost benefit analysis in situations like the south-west forests,' said Harry.

We don't know until three lines later who is speaking. Here's the solution.

'No,' said Harry. 'We have all sorts of professionals talk at our conferences who look at social and economic factors that impact on the environment so we can do some sort of cost benefit analysis in situations like the south-west forests.'

While it is unconventional, placing dialogue tags first is a good way to ensure the reader knows who's talking.

Careful placement of dialogue tags can also change the emphasis of someone's words. Compare the tone of the first line to the second in this example.

'Let's go outside for a walk,' said Hank.

'Let's go,' said Hank, 'outside for a walk.'

In the first line, there is no particular feeling for the way that Hank is speaking, whereas in the second line, the breaking up of his dialogue into two parts gives a feeling that he is speaking in a much more commanding tone.

Minimising Names in Dialogue and Tags

Attributing dialogue tags in a conversation between one male and one female is easy. You just need to use 'said Bill' and 'said Mary' for the first beat of each person, and then drop the names and use 'he' or 'she' occasionally in an action beat to remind the reader who is speaking (e.g. 'She pushed her hair away from her face.')

It gets harder with two or more people of the same gender because you can't use 'he', if they are both men or 'she' if they are both women, so you have to repeat their names at suitable intervals.

If the sequence gets too long, then add in an action beat as well. Here is an example of two men running together. To help with knowing who's who, the occasional action beat and 'said' is included.

> They were silent for a while then Dan said, 'How far does this go?'
> 'All the way into the Adelaide Hills I suppose, though I think to follow the river much further we have to cross over to the other side. Otherwise we'll end up running on roads.'
> Dan pointed up ahead. 'There's a footbridge.'
> After they'd crossed over, Nick said, 'So who's the American?'
> 'What American?'
> 'Katie's squeeze.'
> 'Katie's squeeze?'
> 'Sorry, next question. Read any good books lately?'
> Dan shook his head. 'Had to happen, I suppose, eventually.'
> 'Mate, forget I said anything. My mistake. What book are you reading? I know you like to read.'
> '*The Little Drummer Girl*.'
> 'John le Carré?'
> 'Yeah.'
> 'Any good?'
> 'Yeah, I enjoy spy stories.'
> 'Tell me about it. I don't get much time to read fiction.'

At Stephen Terrace they turned and came back down the far side of the Torrens to King William street, then walked along the footpath into the city.

In the hotel lift Dan said, 'Want to join us for dinner?'

'Thanks mate, but I think Jeremy's expecting me to go somewhere with him, meet his new girlfriend.'

'A scientist?'

'Pseudo scientist.'

'Psychologist?'

Nick laughed. 'You got it.'

For a moment they their eyes met, then Dan said, 'Bitch.'

Nick smiled, though with sadness in his eyes. 'All's fair in love and war I reckon mate.'

'No mate. That's the thing I learned in 'Nam. It's not. Nowhere near it.'

You should also minimise the number of times that one person refers to another person by name. For example:

'Hi Bethany,' said Simon.

'Hi Simon,' said Bethany.

'Bethany, I wondered whether you are going to the meeting this afternoon?'

'No, Simon, I'm not. What about you?'

'I don't think so Bethany, I had hoped you were going and could take some notes for me.'

In this set of dialogue every name can be removed after the second 'Simon' because we know the respondent must be Bethany, plus we don't need any dialogue tags either especially if there is a lead-in sentences that mentions Simon.

Simon looked down from the top of the stairs.

'Hi Bethany.'

'Hi Simon.'

'I wondered whether you are going to the meeting this afternoon?'

'No, I'm not. What about you?'

'I don't think so. I had hoped you were going and could take some notes for me.'

'Sarah said' or 'Said Sarah'?

Is there a difference between 'Sarah said' and 'said Sarah' in dialogue tags? Not really when names are used, but it seems old fashioned now to write 'said she', and so 'she said' tends to be the preferred form. The logical extension of this is that when names are used, the dialogue tags should be 'Sarah said', not 'said Sarah'.

However, a review of some 20 novels from my collection reveals the following: 11 books used 'said Sarah', seven books used 'Sarah said' and two mixed it up. Interestingly, my examination found that dialogue tags are almost non-existent in many recent books, having been largely replaced by character actions. In one book, I found absolutely no dialogue tags whatsoever.

My conclusion is that it doesn't matter whether you use 'Sarah said' or 'said Sarah', but whichever you chose, be consistent throughout your book.

Before or After?

The vast majority of authors put the dialogue tag (if they use one) after the dialogue as shown in all the examples in the sections above. Very occasionally, however, an author will put the dialogue tags first. Here is an example from Alex Miller's book *Journey to the Stone Country*:

> Arner remained so unmoved by her question, so impassive and absorbed in his meal, that he might genuinely have been unaware of her. Trace laughed and looked at Bo.
> Bo said, 'They're down in the contract as field officers.'
> Susan said, 'Dougald's idea, I suppose.'
> [*Journey to the Stone Country* by Alex Miller, Loc: 417 of 4636].

Chapter 6

Remembered, Reported and Inner Dialogue

Recount of Remembered Dialogue

When a POV protagonist is reminiscing, remembered dialogue is sometimes presented in an abbreviated format, without separate lines for each character's dialogue beats. Here is an example from the masterful *Raj Quartet* first volume *The Jewel in the Crown*. In this scene, the POV character, Sister Ludmilla, is remembering a visit by the Chief Superintendent of Police, Ronald Merrick. Her assistant is Mr de Souza and they are talking about a young man who they had found drunk the previous night (Hari Kumar).

> 'Mr de Souza,' I said, 'the boy who spent the night with us –?' And Mr de Souza said casually, 'As you see, he is all right now and making ready to go.' 'I'm afraid no one can go until I say so,' Merrick said, not to me but to the sub-inspector, avoiding cleverly, you see, a direct engagement. 'Are we then all under arrest?' I asked, but laughed, and indicated that arrest or not I wished to conduct him to the third building.
>
> [*The Jewel in the Crown* Book 1 of *The Raj Quartet* by Paul Scott, p.132 of 451].

Alternatively, the dialogue can be recounted without dialogue marks in a loose 'he said, she said' style.

> I asked Mr de Souza about the boy who spent the night with us. And Mr de Souza said casually, as you see, he is all right now and making ready to go. Then I said that Mr Merrick had said, not to me but to the sub-inspector, that no one could go until he said so which was avoiding cleverly, you see, a direct engagement. Then I asked him, are we then all under arrest? But I laughed also and indicated that arrest or not I wished to conduct him to the third building.

[paraphrased from the quote above].

Reported Dialogue

Dialogue can be avoided altogether if the conversation is reported in a narrative style. However, this really only works for short narratives or summaries of a discussion among a group of people.

> Discussion broke out about the circumstances of Wijeweera's death in custody. The latest theory was that the insurgent leader had been taken to a crematorium, shot in the leg and burned alive. Not that anyone really gave two hoots. They were all pleased that the man was dead. It was this impression of a lifting of a pall that lent the party its festive sheen.
>
> [*Questions of Travel* by Michelle de Kretser, p.65].

Narrative dialogue can also be used as a way of introducing a conversation. Here are two examples, again from Michelle de Kretser, an author who seems to have perfected a minimalist approach to dialogue.

> Later that evening, she announced that she wanted to go to Colombo to attend a rally protesting the teargassing of garment workers by the police.
> 'Are you mad?' enquired Carmel. 'Are you asking to be killed or worse?'
> [*Questions of Travel* by Michelle de Kretser, p.115].

> Laura asked if the apple tree outside the kitchen had been planted to replace the lost pear.
> 'I've never eaten such pears as came from that tree. Perhaps there aren't any left in the world.' Theo's hands made a shape. Solid, narrow. A *sculpted* look.
> [*Questions of Travel* by Michelle de Kretser, p.127].

Inner Dialogue

Inner dialogue is very similar to deep third in that the thoughts of the protagonist are revealed, but is done so in a manner that conveys the idea that the person is talking to himself or herself, though not out aloud. Inner dialogue does not need any dialogue punctuation marks. However, if a character is talking out *aloud* to herself, you should punctuate the dialogue as if she is talking to someone else.

When the overall narrative is written in first person, there is no need to change from the use of 'I' and no need for italics.

> I got to a fork in the road. Down the left was a bridge with a barricade. Down the right the forest opened out into fields. Which way should I go? If I went towards the bridge there might be soldiers, though I couldn't see any from where I was standing. But the open fields would expose me to anybody coming up the road. How much time did I have to make a decision? The sound of horses galloping came from behind me. None!

When the overall narrative is written in first or third person, the dialogue can be turned into second person, as if the protagonist was speaking to herself as they would to another person. The self-dialogue can either be in italics or not and, as in the second example provided below, there can be an indication that the person is talking to herself as indicated by the text in brackets which could be part of the sentence depending on your readership. If you have a savvy audience, then leave the text in the brackets out of the sentence.

> I get to the corner store and find myself at the confectionary bar. I am tired. I am feeling sorry for myself. I am cranky after my argument with Sarah. *Don't do it you sucker, don't buy the family bar.* I buy the family bar, the one with milk chocolate and hazelnuts. My favourite. I go home and eat the lot. *You loser. You stupid, piss-weak loser.*

> She went to the window and looked out at the busy street. You are a fool Ms Francis. You are a very stupid fool [she told herself].

Finally, when a character is imagining a conversation with someone else, the other person's dialogue can be put in dialogue marks.

> I arrange my face into something like a look of wry, amused boredom and make a couple of sorties, walking close by her with a nonchalant air, in the hope she'll catch my eye, grab me by the elbow and say, 'Tell me everything about yourself, you fascinating creature.' She doesn't, so I decide to walk by her again.
> [*Starter for Ten* by David Nicholls, p.35 of 338.].

Chapter 7

Punctuating Dialogue

Quotation marks that are used for dialogue (hereafter called 'dialogue marks') differ between English/Australian English and American English in that in English/Australian English single marks ('like these') are used to enclose words of direct speech and in American English double marks ("like these") are used instead (see Section 3.1.8). In all other regards, the rules for punctuating dialogue are the same. In the following examples, I use the English/Australian English system for showing punctuation because I personally believe it is the better system as it wastes less ink and is less busy on the eyes.

The only punctuation marks used for dialogue are:

- single and double dialogue marks
- comma
- full stop (period)
- question mark
- exclamation mark
- em-dash
- ellipsis.

Only One Space

Put only one space between punctuation and words—everywhere—not two. Double spaces between the full stop at the end of one sentence and the capital letter starting the next sentence went out with typewriters. This goes for both dialogue and narrative prose.

All Punctuation Goes Inside the Dialogue Marks

All sentence punctuation goes inside the dialogue marks. This includes full stops, commas question marks and exclamation marks.

Wrong	'I don't know', she said.
Right	'I don't know,' she said.
Wrong	'I think you're wrong'.
Right	'I think you're wrong.'
Wrong	'Do you know'? she asked.
Right	'Do you know?' she asked.

When the Sentence is Continuing After the Tag

If the speaker is continuing her sentence after the dialogue tag, use a comma after the tag and no capital letter for the next piece of dialogue.

Wrong	'I don't think,' she said angrily, 'That this is what should happen.'
Wrong	'I don't think,' she said angrily 'that this is what should happen.'
Wrong	'I don't think' she said angrily 'that this is what should happen.'
Right	'I don't think,' she said angrily, 'that this is what should happen.'

When a New Sentence is Starting After the Tag

If the speaker is starting a new sentence after the dialogue tag, use a full stop at the end of the tag and a capital letter for the next piece of dialogue.

Wrong	'This is madness,' she said to the wizard 'we'll all be trapped.'
Wrong	'This is madness,' she said to the wizard, 'we'll all be trapped.'

Wrong	'This is madness,' she said to the wizard, 'We'll all be trapped.'
Right	'This is madness,' she said to the wizard. 'We'll all be trapped.'

When the Tag Starts the Sentence

If the dialogue tag starts the sentence, put a comma after the introductory phrase or clause.

Wrong	She stamped her foot and said 'This is madness. We'll all be trapped.'
Right	She stamped her foot and said, 'This is madness. We'll all be trapped.'

When the Dialogue is Long

If the dialogue is likely to be a very long sentence, or more than one sentence, insert a dialogue tag after the first convenient phrase or clause, or start the sentence with the dialogue tag.

Wrong	'One summer, when I was about twelve, my father got this crazy idea the family would drive across the Nullarbor for a holiday. It was the classic early-1960s road-trip nightmare. The four of us in an old Holden station wagon. Days and days of eating red dust and flies, and nothing to do but play eye spy. And, believe me, you run out of things to spy pretty quickly driving across a desert,' said Clive.
Right	'One summer,' said Clive, 'when I was about twelve, my father got this crazy idea ...'
Right	Clive said, 'One summer when I was about twelve, my father got this crazy idea ...'

Don't Use Semicolons and Colons

People don't speak in semicolons and colons, so don't put then in dialogue. Use full stops.

Wrong	'I don't know what to do; they could come at any minute.'
Wrong	'I don't know what to do: they could come at any minute.'
Right	'I don't know what to do. They could come at any minute.'

Pauses Require an Ellipsis

Use an ellipsis to indicate when someone pauses in the middle of saying something or tails off into silence. There is no need to state that the person has tailed off though, and note the space between the word and the ellipsis, but not between the ellipsis and the closing dialogue mark.

Right	'I don't know what to do ... maybe I'll tell him.'
Right	'I don't know what to do ...'

Interruptions Require an Em-Dash

Use an em-dash, not a hyphen or en-dash, with no spaces, to indicate when someone has been interrupted.

Wrong	'I don't know what you-' 'What do you mean you don't know?'
Wrong	'I don't know what you–' 'What do you mean you don't know?'
Right	'I don't know what you—' 'What do you mean you don't know?'

Note, there should not be a dialogue tag after interrupted dialogue. If you need one, then put it first.

Wrong	'I don't know what you—' she said. 'What do you mean you don't know?'
Right	She said, 'I don't know what you—' 'What do you mean you don't know?'

Note also, when someone interrupts their own dialogue, the em-dash goes outside the punctuation, not inside.

Wrong	'I don't know—' she searched in her handbag for a tissue '—what he wanted.'
Right	'I don't know'—she searched in her handbag for a tissue—'what he wanted.'

Quote Marks Within Dialogue Marks

Occasionally there is a need to enclose a word or phrase in quotation marks that occurs within dialogue marks. In this instance, use the reverse of whatever is being used for dialogue marks (i.e. if you are using the English/Australian system of single marks, then the internal quotation marks should be doubles; if you are using the American system of doubles, then the internal quotation marks should be singles).

Wrong	'He called him a 'drongo' and laughed,' said Terry.
Wrong	"He called him a "drongo" and laughed," said Terry.
Right	'He called him a "drongo" and laughed,' said Terry.
Right	"He called him a 'drongo' and laughed," said Terry.

If quote marks come at the end of the dialogue, they stay within the dialogue punctuation.

Wrong	'I wasn't the one to call him a "drongo,"' he said.

Wrong	'I wasn't the one to call him a "drongo"', he said.
Right	'I wasn't the one to call him a "drongo",' he said.

Paragraph Breaks in Multiple Paragraph Monologue

When one character speaks for so long that a paragraph break is needed, there is no closing dialogue mark at the end of the paragraph, until the speech ends, but there is an opening dialogue mark at the beginning of the next paragraph to indicate that the same person is still talking.

'Ladies and gentleman,' he started. 'Welcome to Perth. Being some three thousand kilometres from the eastern states, it's one of the most isolated capital cities in the world. This fact alone has led to an intense commitment to self-development over recent years and a goal of continued state prosperity; one which every other state shares I am sure.

'Australia rode on the sheep's back for well over a century, but more recently we've started to ride on the back of the mining industry. ... In other words, the economic growth of this state is inextricably linked to the management of our forests.'

Note, in the example above, there is no closing dialogue mark at the end of the first paragraph after the word *sure*. However, this convention is fading and being replaced by another dialogue beat at the start of the next paragraph. This means that a close dialogue mark would be needed at the end of the first paragraph after the word *sure*, as shown below.

'Ladies and gentleman,' he started. 'Welcome to Perth. [...] development over recent years and a goal of continued state prosperity; one I am sure.'

He took a sip of water from the glass on the lectern. 'Australia rode on the sheep's back for well over a century [...].'

Chapter 8

Omission of Dialogue Marks

The omission of dialogue marks in fiction has been around for over a century. It came into vogue a couple of decades ago[5] but it never really took off for mainstream fiction because it is hard work for readers, trying to keep up with what is dialogue and what is not. You'll find it more often in literary fiction than in genre fiction. Here's an example from Cormack McCarthy's *The Road*:

> When he got back the boy was awake. I'm sorry, he said.
> It's okay.
> Go to sleep.
> I wish I was with my mom.
> He didn't answer. He sat beside the small figure wrapped in the quilts and blankets. After a while he said: You mean you wish that you were dead.
> Yes.
> You mustn't say that.
> [*The Road* by Cormack McCarthy, p.43].

McCarthy gets away with it because for much of the novel there are only two people (a nameless man and his son) and the dialogue between them is sparse. Here's another example, this time from Tim Winton's *Dirt Music* where, again, much of the dialogue is only between two people and is not complicated.

> Just after eight Georgie walked the silent boys to school, kissed their averted heads and walked on to Beaver's to see about a car.
> He seemed surprised to see her. She put a Bette Davis cassette on his counter.
> Not her best, he mumbled.

---

[5] I recall first seeing it in Frank McCourt's autobiography *Angela's Ashes* which was published in 1996.

So what's the gossip?
Industrial deafness. Georgie. Blame. Harley Davidson.
Can you sell me a car?
Not before Christmas. You wanna lift somewhere?
No, I've got a renter for a moment.
Jesus, George.
What?
Be careful .
[*Dirt Music* by Tim Winton, p.128].

An alternative to dialogue marks is the insertion of an em dash before each line of speech. Here is an example from *Ulysses* by James Joyce.

He laid the brush aside and, laughing with delight, cried:
—Will he come? The jejune Jesuit?
Ceasing, he began to shave with care.
—Tell me, Mulligan, Stephen said quietly.
—Yes, my love?
—How long is Haines going to stay in this tower?
Buck Mulligan showed a shaven cheek over his right shoulder.
—God, isn't he dreadful? he said frankly.
[*Ulysses* by James Joyce, loc: 30 of 11,291].

List of References

- *A Division of the Spoils*, Book 4 of *The Raj Quartet* by Paul Scott
- *Caleb's Crossing* by Geraldine Brooks
- *Conditions of Faith* by Alex Miller
- *David Copperfield* by Charles Dickens
- *Dirt Music* by Tim Winton
- *Journey to the Stone Country* by Alex Miller
- *Lady Chatterley's Lover* by D. H. Lawrence
- *Questions of Travel* by Michelle de Kretser
- *Searching for the Secret River* by Kate Grenville
- *Starter for Ten* by David Nicholls
- *The Art of Fielding* by Chad Harbach
- *The Jewel in the Crown* Book 1 of *The Raj Quartet* by Paul Scott,
- *The Road* by Cormack McCarthy
- *The Understudy* by David Nicholls
- *The Wedding Party* by Elizabeth Rose
- *Ulysses* by James Joyce
- *We Need to Talk About Kevin* by Lionel Shriver